PIANO SOLO

IRVING BERLIN

WHITE CHRISTMAS

ARRANGED BY LORIE LINE

Grandma Moses: WHITE CHRISTMAS.Copyright © 1989, Grandma Moses Properties Co., New York

White Christmas

from the Motion Picture, Irving Berlin's HOLIDAY INN

Words and Music by Irving Berlin — *Arranged by Lorie Line*

17
21
25
2
29
33

Like the beginning
37
8va
mp
Verse Two
41
mf
45
49
53

57
61
65
69
73
Verse Three
rit.
f a tempo

76
80
84
88
91
mf

94
97
101
rit.
104
Like the beginning
mp
107
8va
pp

DISTRIBUTED BY
HAL•LEONARD®

$6.95

222 Minnetonka Avenue South
Wayzata, MN 55391
1.800.801.5463 (LINE)
www.lorieline.com

ISBN 978-1-891195-28-0
9 781891 195280
8 84088 54645 8
TLP-390-2
HL00354140